VERT

DUSTIN HELLBERG

POEMS

First published 2023

ISBN 978-981-18-8188-6

Cover and Layout **Sarah and Schooling**
Font **Nudista**

Some of these poems have appeared in the following publications: *Iowa Review*, *Past Simple*, *Cider Press Review* & *Barrow Street Journal*. My thanks to these publishers and editors.

The author would like to thank The Iowa Arts Council and the In and In Law Firm in Seoul, South Korea for generous grants that helped make finishing this book possible.

To *Diane*

there's barely a breath of wind, and no clouds,
and far away from where I hunt
the reindeer graze on the coldblue skyline
they do not see me, and I do not yet see them

— Inuit hunting song

PART ONE

God

It's weird. First you animate the clay. It
smiles at you. What then? So you teach it death,
get no applause. You get mad and cancel health
and recess. You invent work but feel regret,

so you pause. You give it a unicorn
it then fucks and eats. *Where's that unicorn,*
you bellow. It lies. 'It ran away,
but can we have another', asks the clay.

You explain, *I gave you the light and look
what you do in the dark. Where do you get
those ideas? Why is that remote control*

in your ass? Clay says, 'It's all because of death'.
*Can't you just live with it? What if I told
you the secret? In the beginning I took*

You've Never Seen Me Grill a Hotdog Before

The day made everything about sex and
why shouldn't it? The day uses words like
'sluice' and 'kith'. The day dares you to 'be the
you you'. The day is just another perspective

among the many serious ways of
defining perspective, you visitor,
here in the gift shop, here among many
impossible positions of the light

sluicing from body to body, like some
horned-up prankster god's busy hands. The day
says, Did you think she'd stay with you, really?

The day says, Forever. Says, Kith me. Says,
Jump in the water. Says, The body sinks slowly
though it's the heaviest prayer that we have.

A Scientist, Sequencing the Genome of a
Chimp Named Ralph, Speaks

A chimp jumping around in welders' bibs is
funny if not actually welding but sits
& instead writes *The History of Feelings and Arts*.
Think you're Tolstoy? Did you invent sadness

again, Ralph? Can you love two women at once?
Human women? I did & I broke like a child's arm.
So fuck you, Ralph, you don't understand. When I'm
naked my friends call me Tolstoy. We dance.

What do your friends call you? The bed's light & sand
flavored tonight, Ralph. Ralph, give me your hand,
tuck me in, touch me, be my ampersand.
You're 97% me, Ralph, &
what about the rest, the missing 3?
Let's shave you down, monkey, & see what we see.

**'I Like to Use Metaphor and
Multiple Layers of Meaning'**

Break my heart in a new way or buy me
soy milk, but buy it in a heartbreaking way.
Your carbon used to get in the way of my carbon.
The way I'd open your hand expecting

to find a caterpillar growing there.
Vegas' odds were against me taking
off my pants. You hustled like a goddess
in need of a shell-comb before the gods had

invented the body. I lost the pants
bet. Lost your number. The caterpillar
grew up and plagiarized love, got an F.
Your hand on the bus was an elegy,
holding mine, echoed there like sound stretched, stretchir
over you, like a girl stretched over me and all of Mongolia.

Beautiful Ground Zero

What the hell did I know, asking the birds
for a better name for beauty, clearer vocable
than the standard grunt-grunt, twitch-twitch.
I put out bread-loaded hands, thought, *St. Francis*.

How, in another belief the souls of birds
are us, wingless, in a cave, eating floors
made of dust, no bearings bright. The average life
span of a dollar is 14 months, ragged and useless past this

for the vending machines. Where then are your
fingernails now? What was their warranty
but carbon, light, debt, years, a box of switched

receipts. Hold them, they and their syllabary,
translate the currency to birds and bread, a whole
world trilling, *Made in China, Made for Me*.

Pap

The rain lisps as if thirsty for something more
than itself. The way the ladders hang down
from the helicopters that circle the city,
lines of cartoon rain. I am a place
so Paleolithic I make out with stones,
whisper to them, *The world ends every*
day. Bacteria are the master race.
The world is loud. Stick your tongue in my ear.

But there is this woman about to board a flight
so rub some of this on the rash for the pain.
Even on days that fell out of blossom, me & you

so cocky we rhymed plains with Spain and rain
because days there were we grew so rare and light
our selves began to outnumber ourselves.

Cladistics

The skull is screaming at you in the skull your
skull rents: *So-and-So is doing well in
Chicago, Japan*, quotes H. Bogart,
smokes a cigarette and dies. Infinitives
are split. The world splits from excessive praise
like a woman doing splits. Your loss has come
far to greet you, to ask for the money
you borrowed last summer that you spent on
a sheep jaw, horsehair brush, salt, energy drinks.
Loss says, *She never loved you.* It's true,

though I'd like to explain my position:
I have no position, no house, no love
letters to convince your junk to join my
junk, or come out as far as Cho-fu-sa.

Flesh Colored

We got bored and made toast, bored the toast, held
ourselves accountable, then countable,
drank till the wood walls felt accidental
which made the trees sad, & they bent in the wind,

like really nice people bent by misfortune,
like angels in cathedrals on bikes with one
gear, like drunk horses, like death and like reindeer,
like everyone's comma-shaped standing on hills

in a particular wind, particular
place, which I am not at liberty to
tell you, cast in a light that has traveled this
long through literally nothing to show
you your face in this mirror that tells you, Quote:
Your face is a face you'll again never know.

No, You Can't Have Any More Ointment

The ashtray was on fire when I went to
smoke, making it even more literal.
Fire's only trick to make everything literal
with a touch. You told me on the phone you

made hummus, ice jammed the lock, had the flu,
won't be back. Would you like me to barter
for touch? And I'd still give you water
for ashtrays of fire you don't get to choose.

Of all the inhabitants I've ever
been, how strange, now, to be your insurance
against myself, as against every fire
I never set. Would you believe I'm innocent
of conviction, am failed governments
of love, am this moment's spine breaking.

Suicide in Royal We

Hold me up to the light. I will attribute
to you my promises. We must be tried
for treason anyway, that most provincial
of attires. Oblivion, you and your fat, fingered

belly, I love you. I would rather have you
than cartloads of moths and snow and opal.
The small rain returns and there must be worms
in the roses to turn the horizon this color

of color. I think we'll go down to the grey lake
again, clinging to the swollen man, and scull
his well-paddled corpse around for a while
for anyone around who's interested around
for anyone around who's interested around
for anyone around who's interested around

Political Poems Are Dope

.

This is not a political poem, but
there was an old woman, and a girl from
Nantucket. Three pigs came along and dared
you to suck it. Your apartment is cold.
You grow old. You wallet laughs loud at you,
no money to fold. There once was a president,
there once was a shoe. You have no children.
How did that happen? How 'bout a joke? Two
homosexuals walk into a bar
and order one shoe. Will they get married
and live in that shoe? Will they seek therapy,
lawyer up, get divorced? Or will you? Will you
find love like your horoscope says, cuz it's true,
politicians, like hos, gotsta eat too.

A 2 Disc Collection of the Ukrainian
Love Songs of my Youth

The trees over there are pouting in their
grove. *I see dead people*, they say. We know
they mean us and weeds and stars. If you stare
long enough, everything dies. It's slow

this view of history. If you stare long
enough, everything becomes a face. This
proves you're lonely and human. The moon kicks
you in the groin, friendly-like. You belong

to someone else, or did, and because of
that belonging you rode like buffalo
driven from a cliff. You can call love a
causal thing. Trees don't care. The line they stole
from movies you won't watch again, no
matter how girls shine like moons in love.

Milkman XIII

Girls poop, too, now give me a kiss. Take me
to Makeout Creek. I'll be your posture
for sleep, then I'll give you all of Iowa.
I'll paint the cave for you, a scale model
of the cave I'm painting. Any questions?
The difference between *wet computer* and
the heart is the answer to the test
you're not taking. So, anyway, be my

species, LAN line, firewall, my wall of fire,
all the above, pail of milk, my trickle
down economy because all I seem
to do is trickle, seem to taste my tongue
curdle on you. And what if we're imposters,
kiss-tangled wires? Us, sought, lost, frail, fraught.

The Secret of Life

I hope you brought your insurance card, hope
your skin lights up in the dark, hope you have AAA
batteries, hope your pelvis is not a
cardinal direction. I hope you plead

the 5th, didn't forget the Contra code,
have committed the Apocrypha to
memory because it won't be long now.
Did you even have a question? I need

those batteries back. Let's see some ID.
Can I borrow some money for the bus?
What did you think the insurance was for?

I can start the pelvic exam, so please
lie down. I'm ready to tell you the answer:
One by one, death's curing itself of us.

Keep Your Hands Off My
Infinitely Repeating Daughters

When Coyote asks for the boomerang back,
just hand it over. Tell him to please
stick to the nutmeg grove. He sashays around, says,
Doing what I must, and off he walks.

As a dowry he translated the Sumerian
tablets. One read, *A receipt for one dead cow
and two small cattle*. Ever notice how
you staple skin to skin, man to woman,

and no one calls you *doctor*. No requests
for house calls or to taste your medicine.
Your daughters live with Coyote in a shack.
If you love something, set it free. If it
comes back, it was probably a boomerang.
Where'd Coyote been hiding it? Don't ask.

Morality

Why salt, natron, juniper oil, why all
these lists sewn up to sky, the the, slurry
of a day's dehisce beaten back to innocence.
Let gravity do its work on your name

and watch the wick go saint, go out, and blame
the person you're not for where you've been,
what all your crosseyed family did and were.
No one comes and says, Hey, it's not your fault,

nor will they. Life's a fizzled knot and stitch. When
I had surgery they stopped my heart with rain
forest frog venom, slough of green and orange

synthesized epidural neurotoxin,
and imagine being so beautiful the world
had to give you a bright and poisonous skin.

Stuff and Procedures I'd Like
to Name After Myself

Hannibal, Missouri, for one. How to
cure cancer. How to warm the alphabet
or warn it. How to shave you, and to vet
the hot tubs. I'd clone the world in yellow

and rhyme everything I saw with apogee.
If I'm being honest, I'm lying. Ha.
You already knew the words woulda
coulda. That woman was water once to me.

And now not. I named myself Hannibal,
forgot her lopsided teeth. I forgot
the giraffes, Seoul, the jab of sloths. I lost

the how to, all over her, climb on top.
How to patent the past. How to. How to.
Full stop. Full stop. Full stop. Full stop. Full stop.

To a Friend Long Unheard From, From My Backyard in Late Spring

Far owned and under, daffodils don masks
of cloud. A bruise as slow as truth calls down
through memory of a river's name you
stood at once, crying, in a different life.

Do you remember the rowboat, your shirt
off while I pulled at oars as sure as your arms
pulled me later? You were the saint of hours.
Now, there is no town to drive to, no wife

to dance a tongue on. No. Explain the ash
on my lawn as something more than fire's dew.
Some kids, learning play again, zip on bikes
by. Honey laughter pours. The sun is warm.

Don't worry, friend, you always hate the lawn
you have to mow when the grass isn't yours.

Knuckle Sandwich

Here's what's on the test: The smell of fresh-cut
lawn is really the grass' pheromones
screaming. If you shoot an elephant in
your pajamas, blame Groucho or Karl.

Take a knee is not meant to be literal.
In one box, Schrödinger's cat is dead.
In another, it has stolen your wife.
She sends postcards from Bimini: *The cat's*

sunburnt and lost. I know what you're thinking.
I know you won't lick my wounds again. That's
what she said. That's just science. I know salt's

your secret ingredient. Your grass is blooming.
I can see you through the windows. I
can tell you're dying without even looking.

The Year That I Wasn't Married

was like the other years, but different, like
that dream where you're wearing a house not wearing
its pants, but it's not your house, then someone gives
you back the ring, gives your mom cancer, your

best friend leaves you for her husband, and then
everyone's an armadillo rolling
to different rental units. Someone gives
you cancer, and everything rattles loose.

Consider what rattles loose yours. Finders.
Consider the whale, consider the crocus.
Consider the quadrangle. Consider
the lark. Consider me yours. Consider
me gone. Consider my body a body
of theory why I didn't, or don't, or do.

Knot

horse/fingers//singe/rose

jawbone/grass//borne/rags

shape/lament//petal/ash
slate//slate
angelus/stone//shore/kneel

outward/bloom//towards/toward

song/no//go/sing

Say something warm. Hello. The world
was full of harm until this wind
placated grass and put the fish to rest.
And wave hello. Someone may be out there
riding undulating light our way.

—Richard Hugo

PART TWO

Adjusted for Inflation

Museum food court. We just saw Egyptian
bas-reliefs, the baskets and reed shoes. There's
a half-eaten $12 sandwich on
a plastic plate. Glass breaks. Her, turning,

in profile, always elsewhere, a turning
from the now, this single point perspective,
cost of admission. Chicago's all eyes.
Love's as rare as rust. The Pharaoh is always

Pharaoh-sized, she says. The slave is always
the size of today. We all have one good eye
in profile. The crocodile god says nothing.

Hearts and feathers on the scales weigh nothing
at all, like me, her, and those eternal, two
dimensional, weightless, dead Egyptians.

Chicxulub

I checked the forecast, found fissures and light.
No strike predicted from comet or meteor.
How lucky. But sixty six million years
ago, some 95% of life

just went. Had Earth been ahead four minutes
or behind in orbit, that rock would have whizzed
right by, tumbleweed that the car just missed.
Now, imagine the weather a comet

makes. Imagine the ghost of a dinosaur
chewing on the ghosts of plants. How lonely.
How Saturn's rings look solid till you get

close, find rocks, tumbling in the black, ghostly,
locked in a very cold place and very
empty, orbiting weather as deep as a planet.

Upon Hearing that His Former Lover
Has Taken Another Lover Lover Lover

Perhaps the world was always a photo
copy on a parachute, slow controlled descent
through the patience and the feedings, colors
that stitch moment to moment to moment.

Her father hurt her and her mother died.
I held her. There's a yellow chill, wide as
love. What I mean is death, how it snaps
its yellow teeth, spits, then smiles. Now she hides

behind forever. The world was wider than
the desert's songs. I am bewildered. I'd
not beg her back. Sometimes I think I would.

A lifetime is water and screaming, then
you're gone. Sometimes staying drunk is best.
You fly home to dead parents. Then you rest.

**Baby Elephant Plays in Waves
While Birds Watch with Envy**

Why all these birds inside me? The lesbians
next door might know, with their Mickey Mouse
t-shirts. So, I buy them toilet paper,
leave it at their gate. It's not their house

I envy, but their cat they've named after
a cigarette, Chicago or Seoul,
I think. A woman and me, once pressed in
bodies, watched each other from private folds.

I've watched all the silent films in Korean.
Nights, I count the DVD's that I've stolen
from friends, the beauty, water wheels, airfare,
summer smell of fireworks among the cedars,
baby elephant splashing. I do that to
remember who I am, & why the birds die where they do.

Tectonics

They have predicted an earthquake soon. The beasts
in this cracked desert of one season don't
seem to know. Neither fled nor silent in
a sunrise the color of agate, days

always the color of sand in your teeth
from oceans you will never visit. Didn't
the torn page I found this morning resting
against my tire mean something in its fading,

picture of a woman's splayed legs, my own Iseult
sweet in dawn's lux, saying, *Here is your envelope of anthrax. Here
is your heartbeat of glass shutting over every moment like a vise in that over-plied council
of this body, and yours and yours and yours, in the raking gazes of the carcasses stumbling
inside the carcass and those things moving inside us, afloat on a sea of fire,
such force, such stuff, continental but drifting.*

My God, It's Full of Bacon

Dear future cadaver, why do you walk
along the beach, trailing your strings, your past's
attachments, past loves and bodies crass
as salt? You're insane, nervous as compass

needles. Some assembly is required, followed
by much disassembly. Cadaver, talk
a little. You're not as useful as horse
hooves for glue. Believe me, I've tried.

Tried every fix and cure. Every part must
be used. Nothing wasted. Cadaver, I might
be losing it. But I could still make a kite

out of you, take you to the beach and cast
you in wind. Take flight. Take the freeway west.
Send letters. Feel useful, loved. Lonely and alive.

Die Billige Winterhute des Schicksals

Here we go, dopplering across and down
the universal blah blah blah. Because my
choices are small facts and then mistakes it
made me think of cruelty and the ocean.
Tulle from old French for 'plated armor'.
Or saunter, *santus terrus*, 'to holy land'.
Or muslin, *mawshil*, which is to join together.
Or seersucker, from the Persian, *shir*

u shakar, 'milk and sugar, milk and sugar'.
Feel around for a better place to sleep.
The stone in your heart. Mimic the bird
calls, ammunition of the deep forests.
Easily, easily that ocean. Harder the fabrics
of hunger and fact. Yours if you want them.

Kevin Costner Plays Randy 'Big Unit' Johnson in a New Biopic

Physics asks that we trust chalk on the board
and the pinch hitter. Summer drinks are theorems
that eventually explain God, the zeroes
in your bank account, your student loan defaults.
Fiction's on the mound. The grass is greener
than you recalled. Kevin's yelling *Daddy*
Daddy Daddy somewhere out in the dark.
Kevin long ago fled from language to

the department of not needing people
or their genitals. Here is the record
of all the numbers Kevin learned to count:
first, second, third. It's raining now. Kevin
long ago resigned himself to Kevin,
to live comfortably on his student loans.

Randy 'Big Unit' Johnson as a Metaphor for Kevin

Johnson was, once, slang for penis. 'Why not
Kevin?', cried Kevin who called his agent
and asked for more scripts. The role would require
field research. He hid under the bleachers
and watched kids make out on their phones. It scared
him how distant he felt. Kevin called out
for Jesus, for his mother, for some goddamn
decent guac. The sky flared. A voice called down:
Have you heard the one about Moses and
the Burning Bush? Jesus stepped out from
behind the bleachers. *Yes, Kevin, I am*
the father of all, everything,
even your crabs. Kevin told Jesus, 'Let's
play ball', and took him as far as second base.

Gordian

A halo forms around the street lights: water
ruthless as nature and graph: shibboleth
of photon: and underneath the light you sit:
knot of hands, insect in amber.

A crow can talk if you cut its tongue in half,
but what would it speak of, the forked
ends' split-root like grass shoots tasted, shorter
than the questions you failed to ask:

Fields of twist, how people play life, or it's
because we cannot predict love-sick teens
or Stalin, great intellects that explain
spiders and fish now extinct, feints

in advance of you like Zeno's arrow:
helix and here's end, zero and error.

Hamartia

In Korea, once, a man the size of his
skeleton, buying a generic can
of beans, counted the smallest coins on
the counter while behind him you waited

in line to buy some butter. Remember
that guy who stabbed you with a boxcutter
in Eagle, Colorado? That other
time you beat two men senseless? It all blurs,

Utah to California, and later
Korea. You learned enough words to order
a beer or the taxi left/right. Back to the store

and the line where you were buying butter,
where you could have bought an old man's dinner
for him, and you didn't. God damn me, I didn't.

The Boötes Void

For J.H.

All our dead friends are a symptom. The way
they crosshatch Earth. They're now elemental,
all so literally elemental,
their carbon unfolding. Fleet territory

this monkey-collage called Human. Debris
so final like the tide brings and takes. There's
a void in the universe, no galaxies,
nothing. This is where dead friends gather

and gossip about us. Who's going to take
that from them? You'll only mistranslate their sky.
The version you are will vanish in a lake

of fire and dark. Dead friends laugh when we cry:
Good dog, good boy, good gods, good night, good bye
my friend who died last week whose name was Jake.

Climates Change

Grey morning rain. And there it hangs, water
droplet on a green leaf's edge. A world it
inverts parallaxes behind and around it
where crude facts crash like markets and river
water burns. Light coughs weather up and scours
ash for explanation. That droplet is
the edge of gravity, is fugitive,
an emulsion like a photograph of stars,

geometries of movement bent, such things
that send the mornings singing, grey that swerves
to view. What's the world but a thing to live in
as parent, child. Here, all the water brings.
The morning's grey. That drop dilutes then dims
and breaks a great, cracked world to curve.

Matchbook

Houses hive on Korean hills. I run
up Namsan Mountain toward the incense
burning at the temple. It's cruel, that hill,
on calves. Say it's for my health. And Korean's

just a word I'd mutter on top a mountain,
and what's a word except a shrine on fire,
each new utterance proof that to speak builds
and then destroys. I pray the gods murder

the heavens, crawl down and murder me with
lightning or a hymn, or would pull the sun
through ozone, burn the world to true again.

Where's this poem going? What am I bid?
My tears are real as worlds I won't give back
unless you set your mouth on fire, laugh, and ask.

Plinth

The hummingbird swooped, touched my flowered shirt-
and me stock-still on the back porch. The hum
and then absentium of it, amid the hull-
abaloo of Hawaiian print and girth

of California, and the girl inside
the apartment who'd eventually steal
my clothes and money. Well, the shit got real
as the saying goes, or went, or did. Besides,

I am so sick of burth and birial,
the hummingbird is as long as its tongue,
and she can have the money, and no meal

my shirt, so the dart-bird flew, hungry and dumb,
like everyone away, away, like all
our body a'comet saying, *Come, come*

Self Portrait with Gravity

Remember that day we squared the circle,
marched the horizon down to math? That day
we watched the bee drown, you placed a veil
over the bread, called your hands veils, and touched

everything. What I want to tell you now:
I vouch that all the feet will turn your way.
Back, it's a long walk to the house you've borrowed.
Combined, they were a grass rope we followed

when our arms were tanned, fields full of myrtle
and stammer. The bee is dead, veils fall slouch
where there's never enough time for music

flown of its landscape like a paper gown,
when the flowers bloomed to earth like slow fuses
and the air followed you all the way down.

Green Kickers

Everyone has one and then they don't, a
mother. The last time I saw her was
on a screen while my sister held the computer.
I was in Korea, they in Iowa.

Already bad, her vision couldn't clear
through morphine and cancer, but then she smiled
and reached a hand to a me that wasn't there.
But I was, Mother, and am. Am a first

last word now, a list made of lists, childish
first step across a lullaby of nerves,
scatterings of tiny teeth, oceans of

birth, density of skies that all rhyme with
that song you sang me once, *you are my sun
shine you are my sunshine you are my sun*

After she died I traveled home and built
a dam back in the woods. First rain it washed
out, creek running its banks. I surveyed it
that night, with the fireflies all ablaze.

Light speaking to light, a language not mine.
I stood there. I was a spectrum of meat.
Drove places. Fixed a friend's doors to open.
Watched river do its thing to banks. Call its

color rubble, meat or neighbor. Just don't
call it what it is. I picked up your death
certificate because Dad said he can't.

Data and names on paper I couldn't read.
Would you like to know what the fireflies said?
I picked up your death I picked up your death.

Sharko, my friends' daughter's pet goldfish died.
I was housesitting that summer. I swear
I fed him, swear I took him for walks, cried
when he cried, loaned him that cup of sugar

he asked for. But that way that goldfish do,
he did. Us, too, I guess, and all our fins,
a sudden grey, and not the gold of smiles
or deeper veins of losses which for miles

burrow in the teeth. Fish are all teeth. When
friends' daughter learned of his demise she said,
Well, he lived longer than I expected.

Good outlook she had for someone who's six.
My Mom's teeth fell out from chemo like lead,
fell out like fish we drop in porcelain.

If it's any consolation (it's not),
I'm mortal too. My knee is bad. I smoke
too much. Same thing got you. What is that joke
repeated so much it's not funny? What

was the punchline but life? Is that why there
was no funeral? You didn't want us
to grieve a body made joke by body's
final dirty song? I'm not laughing here,

don't sing. They burned the joke, boxed your ashes
in cardboard, said they were sorry. I'm not
laughing. How much does fire cost? What are we
but the funeral of a joke told too flat,
too often, too long. It leaves you and me.
It leaves you wondering which laugh is last.

Pergola. Dad and I built a pergola
for you in the woods. We wrapped it in some vines
that withered and fell. I'm half orphan, Ma,
now. Year prior, you drove out to Pike's

Peak by yourself, where mountains shove mountain
so sky can gnaw the stone. There you remain
an altitude I can understand or find.
In Iowa you're ash. Directions blind

the mood of maps. If I could I'd quash
the mountains flat, I'd forgive the water's
failure with the vines. Only water's free

to fail so much. Who says water is
a universal solvent has never watched
a dissolving mother grow tired and light, and cease.

The animal holds onto animal.
We call this love. It happened to me once.
Days fill with the have happened. Paradise
with its revolving door. Maybe I will

get it right next time. Paradise, I mean.
Poverty's a lonely animal to
live. If it rained ash or fish tomorrow,
I'd say I told you so. I'd say I meant

I love those afternoons of stars and birds,
an element like birth. We're all downstream
from where we'll die, the body dowsing home.

The river's drunken dialect is heard
best on nights like this. An animal holds
another, shining golden as the moon.

Dying, she said they stood in the corners,
the Green Kickers, robed in white. She said *They'll
hold death back. It's outside the window near
the bed.* When you're on that much morphine you'll

see and say such things. Can't be helped. They get
names like Vermont or Vermeer. She said they
told her their names but soon forgot. It's not
important. They never turned around. Why

the corners, why the robes? Another
name for dying's *mother*. And what is light
except a corner showing the way home.

Mother is an element, and mother
means no more. Bodies stand in corners, bright
as fire, green as years, whispering our names.

Dustin Hellberg is the author of three other books and many academic articles. He holds doctorates in English literature and philosophy of science, and he received his master's in poetry from the Iowa Writers' Workshop.